Celebrate Passover
HAGGADAH

A Christian Presentation
of the Traditional Jewish Festival

Joan R. Lipis

Purple Pomegranate Productions

Special thanks to Ron Allen and John Kohlenberger III for their
inspiration and encouragement in putting this book together.

Purple Pomegranate Productions, San Francisco 94102

Published 1993. Second Edition 1996
Printed in the United States of America
01 00 99 98   5 4 3 2

Front cover photo by Terry Korotkin
Back cover photo by David Hessimer
Cover design by Patricia C. Holland
Seder Plate photo by Pavel Bosak

Library of Congress Cataloging in Publication Data

Lipis, Joan R.
  Celebrate Passover Haggadah.

  Bibliography: p.
  1. Passover - Christian observance. I. Haggadah
II. Title
1996   93-18254
ISBN 1-881022-23-4   Paperback

This second edition is adapted from the
Passover Feast by the same author.

⋙ FOREWORD ⋘

by Moishe Rosen
Executive Director
Jews f☆r Jesus

God spared Israel from the last plague upon Egypt in the time of Moses. The specter of death bypassed or passed over the households that had followed God's instructions to apply to the doorposts the blood of a sacrificial lamb. The Lord wants this ancient redemption experience to have a lasting effect on all of his people, even believers today.

Yet how can a people best remember history? Books and scrolls primarily capture the interest of scholars; in time, words can lose their meaning. God, the master teacher, devised the perfect method of remembrance. He commanded the annual reenactment of that first Passover night, a ceremony that would appeal through the senses to each person of every generation. Even as we teach little children today through object lessons, YHWH took everyday acts of seeing, hearing, smelling, tasting and touching and made them his allies in teaching holy truths to his people.

God commanded the annual memorial of the Passover observance so that his people might reflect regularly upon all that he had done for them. They were to rehearse and retell the events of the great redemption he had brought to their fathers. They were to rejoice in his past and present blessings and look forward to what he would yet do for and through them.

What God did for the Jewish people at Passover is recounted in what is called the seder. The Haggadah tells what to do at a Passover seder or meal. It also tells the how and why of the seder. Haggadah is Hebrew for "telling" or "showing forth." It is the same root used in Exodus 13:8: "And thou shalt shew thy son in that day" (NKJ). We find the same connotation in the Greek where the Apostle Paul, in describing the Last Supper, writes, "As often as ye eat this bread and drink this cup, ye do shew the Lord's death till he comes" (1 Corinthians 11:26, NKJ). Significantly, the Last Supper was a Passover meal.

Passover has been celebrated in one way or another since the days of Moses. It has evolved through the centuries, with the first order of service being written around 300 AD. Today there are dozens of variations of the Haggadah in publication. The one you hold has been compiled by Jewish believer in Y'shua (Jesus), Joan Lipis. It is for Jewish followers of Y'shua **and** for Gentile Christians. It is especially

3

written for people who have never before participated in or led a seder.

Some people might be concerned that by entering into such a celebration, we violate the spirit of God's grace. After all, the Apostle Paul rebuked the Galatians for insisting that non-Jews had to follow the Law.

This book is not an admonition to Christians to observe the Passover or any part of the Law. It is an opportunity to discover the path of God's greater grace. It is an occasion to experience the depth of the meaning of the Lamb of God whose blood was shed for each of us at Calvary.

This Haggadah brings Christ into the Passover seder, revealing the fulfillment of the coming of the Messiah, the deliverer whom Jewish people through the ages have awaited.

If Miss Lipis in her writing helps you love Jesus more, celebrate the salvation you have in Calvary, sense the redemption through grace, then she has accomplished her purpose.

Let us now celebrate our redemption. Let us rejoice in liberty.

You may contact Joan Lipis at:
Novea Ministries
P.O. Box 16211
Portland OR 97216
503-239-8032
e-mail: JoanRLipis@aol.com

Jews for Jesus may be contacted at:
60 Haight Street, San Francisco CA 94102-5895
e-mail: jfj@jews-for-jesus.org
www.jews-for-jesus.org

⤏INTRODUCTION⤟

This book is a Haggadah. For the Gentile, that is a mouthful; for the Jewish person it is what Grandpa pulled out, dusted off and read every year at Passover. The Haggadah contains the liturgy used in celebrating the traditional Jewish Passover (seder).

You don't have to be Jewish to celebrate Passover or to participate in the seder. It is true that in the seder Jews reenact the time when God delivered their ancestors from bondage to Pharaoh. As Christians, this is also part of our spiritual heritage as revealed in the Old Testament. But as you will see in this Haggadah, Passover can also honor and celebrate Y'shua (the Jewish way to say Jesus) as Messiah. The observance of Passover is based on the requirements specified in the Torah, the five books of Moses (particularly in Exodus 12; Leviticus 23:4-8; Numbers 28:16-25; Deuteronomy 16:1-8), and in Jewish tradition (especially the tractate Pesachim in the Mishnah and Talmud). Our observance will also show how Jesus the Messiah fulfills the salvation message of Passover—and how he delivers each one of us from bondage to sin. Moreover, the Last Supper was a Passover meal (or seder) (Matthew 26:17-30; Mark 14:12-26; Luke 22:7-38; John 13-17; 1 Corinthians 11:17-34) celebrated by Y'shua and his followers. For a full description of Passover read, *Christ in the Passover* by Moishe Rosen (Moody Press).

HOW TO CONDUCT YOUR SEDER

It is easy to prepare for a Passover seder. Certain elements must be included, but there is also a lot of freedom to choose what you will include. You can make modifications to meet your particular budget, needs and preferences.

A seder can be conducted with either a small group in your home or with a larger group in a fellowship hall. It lasts approximately three hours. The first hour retraces the victory of the past, and the last hour looks forward to the future victory when Messiah will come back to claim His people. The meal is eaten during the middle hour. If you find that your service is running long, you may omit those prayers and responsive readings indicated by an asterisk.

At each seder the leader reads from a Haggadah. The Haggadah you hold in your hands has been written for Christians—both Jews and Gentiles who know Y'shua as their Messiah. You will notice that, in this Haggadah, the Christian understanding of the liturgy is explained through the words of the instructor. Everything else carefully follows the Jewish ritual.

Everyone gets involved with the seder, therefore it helps if each person has a copy of the Haggadah.

As you conduct your seder, have fun. It is meant to be a celebration. It is designed to be a living drama, to be experienced each time. Hopefully you will feel some of the excitement and awe of the first Passover in Egypt and the Passover seder in the upper room in Jerusalem.

FACILITY

A seder can be conducted with either a small group in your home or a larger group in a church fellowship hall. It is a festive occasion, so be as lavish as you wish in your decorations.

PARTICIPANTS

Everyone gets involved.

Leader: This person reads the traditional Jewish portions from the Haggadah. He or she leads the service and demonstrates various symbolic acts during the seder. For large groups, it works best if the leader sits or stands at a raised demonstration table during the liturgy and then joins the guests during the meal.

Instructor: This person reads the Christian explanations and prophetic fulfillments of various passages in the Passover service. For large groups, this person also sits at the demonstration table during the liturgy and joins the guests during the meal.

Hostess: Usually the lady of the house (it must be a female), the hostess lights the candles. For large groups, have a hostess for each table.

Host: This person is needed for large groups only. He or she demonstrates the various acts of the seder (such as washing of hands) and helps serve food to the people at his or her table.

Children: Usually the youngest child who is able to read asks the four questions in the Maggid segment of the seder. With large groups, four different children can do the reading.

The Group: There are passages in the Haggadah for the group to read, usually in response to something the leader says.

MUSIC

You will sing several times during the seder. The traditional song "Dayenu" must be sung at the indicated point. Go ahead, give the Hebrew lyrics a try. The words and music are included in the back of this Haggadah. At other times select songs that reflect the liturgy and that are familiar to your group.

FOOD

The Passover seder is a meal as well as a service. The following items can often be found in traditional seder meals. However, you are not limited to these dishes. Feel free to vary them (except for the seder plate elements) according to your budget and personal tastes. **However, do not serve ham or bread.** If you want to prepare the food for your seder using traditional Jewish recipes you can refer to Melissa Moskowitz's booklet, *Passover Recipes* ($1.95, Purple Pomegranate Productions, 80 Page Street, San Francisco, CA 94102).

Appetizer: Gefilte fish served with hot, red horseradish can be purchased ready-made. Chicken soup with matzoh balls. A plate of finger food, which can include carrots, celery sticks, pickles, radishes and olives. You may want to try a common Passover dish such as beet borscht.

Dinner: Include a main dish, vegetables and a dessert. Lamb is often used in smaller seders. Some larger groups prepare one leg of lamb to give everyone a taste. Chicken is a good red meat alternative. Any vegetable will be appropriate. Matzoh pancakes or matzoh blintzes make good dishes. And for dessert, you may want to try a Passover nutcake or carrot ginger candies. Recipes for each of these dishes are contained in *Passover Recipes,* but you can feel free to use your own recipes for your seder.

Wine: The use of wine is discretionary. In many Jewish homes it is expected that wine will be served at Passover as a symbol of our freedom from slavery. However, due to the abuse of wine in our society, it is understandable if you choose not to serve any alcoholic beverage. I also realize that some people have theological reservations about the use of alcohol. Perhaps you might consider using a non-alcoholic wine or a sparkling cider.

TABLE SET-UP

Small groups may want to use nice china. Large groups can use paper tablecloths, napkins, plates and bowls. Each individual should have a complete setting. Any color scheme is acceptable.

Two candles should be on each table. The candles will be lit during the service, so it is advisable that the candles be pre-lit to prepare the wick. Also have matches available.

INCLUDE ON THE TABLE
(in addition to regular settings):

- one seder plate
- one plate of boiled eggs, 1/2 for each person
- small bowls (two for every two participants)

one of plain water for hand-washing
(identify by floating sliver of lemon)
one of salted water for dipping greens
(identify by floating sprig of parsley)
- matzoh tosh (container for three matzot)
you can purchase a ready-made matzoh tosh or you can use a
large dinner napkin; place matzot inside the folds of the napkin
- afikoman bag
- plate of extra matzot
- dish of extra charoset (2 Tbs/person)
- decanter of wine (grape juice can be substituted)
- decanter of water

THE SEDER PLATE

Each table needs a seder plate with enough of the elements to serve each person. Seder plates can be purchased or a large white dinner plate can be used.

The plate includes:
- lamb shankbone (shoulder bone, which you can get from a butcher)
- roasted egg (put boiled egg into warm oven for 8 minutes until brown. Watch out, they sometimes explode!)
- parsley (one sprig for each participant)
- maror: horseradish root, white onion, bitter lettuce or ground red horseradish (one of these items)
- charoset (see recipe on opposite page)
- red ground horseradish or more maror

Charoset Recipe
2 tart apples
1/2 cup walnuts
1/4 teaspoon cinnamon
1 teaspoon honey
1 tablespoon sweet Passover wine

Core apples (it is not necessary to peel them). Chop apples and walnuts together in food processor or blender, or by hand, until finely chopped. With a wooden spoon, stir in the cinnamon, honey and wine. This will serve 10-12 people.

NOTE ON SHOPPING FOR SEDER ITEMS

All Jewish synagogues carry Passover products and are open to the public. Many supermarkets and some specialty stores carry the basics: matzoh, gefilte fish, cake mixes, cookies and candies. The Passover matzot, the candles, cups and other elements can also be purchased from Purple Pomegranate Productions.

SPECIAL INSTRUCTIONS FOR LARGE GROUPS

If you are celebrating the seder as a fellowship group or a church, then you will need to organize yourself. Don't set a head table, rather set up a demonstration table. The leader and the instructor should be seated at this table during the service. When the meal is served, they should join the guests.

The Demonstration Table: As indicated above, the table should be set in such a position that it is clearly visible to all participants. The demonstration table should be set the same as the other tables with the addition of an extra place setting and empty chair for Elijah the prophet. (A place for Elijah is necessary for both large and small groups.) You will need a seder plate and candlesticks. Also include a pitcher and bowl for the "washing of the feet."

PRONUNCIATION

Part of the seder service is done in the Hebrew language. The transliteration is phonetic, approximating sounds rather than formally representing Hebrew letters. All consonants are pronounced as in English except for the "ch." The "ch" should be pronounced as a hard "h" or soft "k" as in the German "Ba<u>ch</u>." Vowels and diphthongs are as follows:

<u>ah</u> as in sh<u>ah</u>   <u>ee</u> as in b<u>ee</u>
<u>ai</u> as in <u>ai</u>sle   <u>i</u> as in p<u>i</u>n
<u>ay</u> as in d<u>ay</u>   <u>oh</u> as in <u>Oh</u>!
<u>e</u> as in m<u>e</u>t   <u>u</u> as in t<u>oo</u>th

BE BLESSED AS YOU CELEBRATE

Your seder is more than a Jewish tradition with a Christian twist. Take time to reflect on the wondrous words and mighty acts of God as revealed through the prophets so long ago. When you do, this reenactment will not only come alive, but you will look forward with greater anticipation to the final fulfillment of prophecy in these latter days.

May Y'shua be exalted and blessed through your Passover seder!

⇚⇒ORDER OF SERVICE⇐⇚

BEDIKAT CHAMETZ (Searching for Leaven)
> Signifies that all bread products and leaven (chametz) have been removed and the home is now prepared for Passover

CALL TO WORSHIP
> Focuses our hearts to God and the purpose of the celebration

BIRKAT HA-NER (Blessing Over the Candles)
> Separates (sanctifies) the evening as a celebration unto God

KADDESH (Blessing of the Meal)
> Separates (sanctifies) this meal as a memorial to God's miracles of the Passover in Egypt
>> "Four Cups": explains the four cups that will be used
>> "The Cup of Sanctification": drinking of the first cup

URCHATZ (Washing the Hands)
> Ritual cleansing in preparation to eat

KARPAS (Eating of Greens)
> Symbolizes renewal through rebirth

YACHATZ (Breaking the Matzoh)
> Remembers the bread of affliction
> Hiding the "afikoman," to be shared later

MAGGID (Recounting the Exodus Story)
> Four Questions: recognizes the difference of this celebration
> Four Sons: symbolizes different attitudes to God's salvation
> Ten Plagues: recounts the plagues God brought on Egypt
> Dayenu: recounts God's many acts of kindness
> The Three Essentials: Pasach/Matzoh/Maror
> The Cup of Deliverance: commemorates deliverance from Egypt

RACHTZAH (Washing the Hands)
MOTZI, MATZOH, MAROR, KORECH (Eating the elements)
> Motzi: blessing the matzoh
> Matzoh: eating the matzoh
> Maror: eating the matzoh with bitter herb
> Korech: eating combination of matzoh, maror and charoset
> Eating the egg: symbolizes destruction of the Temple

SHULCHAN ORECH (Table Is Spread)
Eat the meal
Remember the Passover meal of Messiah
Dramatic Reading: Isaiah 53 and Psalm 22

TZAPHUN (Retrieving the Afikoman)
Introduces first element of communion

BARECH (Blessing for the Meal)
The Cup of Redemption: commemorates God's plan of
redemption, second element of Communion
Elijah's Place: recognizes work and warnings of Elijah

HALLEL (Songs of Praise)
Psalms 115-118, 136 continues to affirm faith in God
Cup of Praise: exalts God for His salvation from Egypt and
from sin

NIRTZAH (Our Observance Is Accepted)
Completes Seder
Next Year in Jerusalem: calls for Messiah's speedy return

*66**T**his is a day you are to
commemorate; for the
generations to come you
shall celebrate it as a festival to the
LORD—a lasting ordinance"*
—Exodus 12:14

⤙⤜ BEDIKAT CHAMETZ ⤛⤞

Searching for Leaven

Leader: As it is written in Exodus 12:14-20, in preparation for the Passover, God commanded the people of Israel to remove all leaven or yeast (in Hebrew chametz) from their houses.

*Adult #1: This simple command has developed into a major and important ritual in preparing for the Passover. The house is thoroughly cleansed, and then the evening before the seder the following prayer is recited:

*Adult #2: Blessed are you, O LORD our God, King of the universe, who has commanded us about removing leaven.

*Adult #3: A search is made with a candle and a feather to ferret out any piece of leaven that might defile the house and therefore the seder. All bread or leaven found is wrapped together and the following prayer is said:

*Adult #4: All leaven or leavened bread in my possession that I have not seen, nor removed, nor known about, is annulled and is useless, like the dust of the earth.

*Adult #1: In the morning the leaven is burned and a similar prayer is recited.

Instructor: It is from this concept of the cleansing of leaven that Paul wrote in First Corinthians 5:6: "Don't you know that a little yeast works through the whole batch of dough? Get rid of the old yeast that you may be a new batch without yeast."

Leader: Let us search ourselves for any leaven, for any impurity of thought, word or deed that might separate us from the presence and peace of God. The Spirit searches all things, even the deep things of God.

*Group: O Lord, you have searched me and you know me. Before a word is on my tongue, you know it completely, O LORD. Search me, O God, and know my heart; test me and know my anxious thoughts. See if there is any offensive way in me that needs to be removed as the leaven was removed from the house. Lead me in your everlasting way.

*Leader: When we confess our sins, he is faithful and righteous to forgive us and to cleanse us from all unrighteousness.

*Group: Let the words of my mouth and the meditation of my heart be acceptable in your sight, O LORD, my strength and my redeemer.

Music: "Create in Me a Clean Heart" or a song of your choice

⋘⋗°CALL TO WORSHIP⋙⋖⋗

Leader: O God, we come to you recognizing you are the source of all we have and all we are. We have set apart this night to remember your mighty acts as you preserved and protected us. You have given yourself to all who believe in you. We rest in your love, your sovereignty, your judgment and your redemption. We declare our faith in you as did our fathers before us.

Instructor: Believers in Y'shua can rejoice:

Group: We rejoice that through your son you have freed the world from the bondage of sin, ignorance and idol worship.

*Adult #1: In the presence of loved ones and friends, and with the symbols of festive rejoicing before us, we gather now for our sacred celebration. With the household of Israel, and all who call themselves by your name, Father God, we are linked with the past and bonded with the future.

*Adult #2: We heed the divine call to service. In word and deed we relive the story that has been told so that all people might see its shining fulfillment in the person and presence of Messiah. As we gather to observe the Passover, we recall your command in Exodus 12:17:

*Adult #3: "Celebrate the Feast of Unleavened Bread, because it was on this very day that I brought your divisions out of Egypt. Celebrate this day as a lasting ordinance for the generations to come."

Leader: We remember the day on which the Jewish people went forth from Egypt, from the house of bondage, and how you freed our Jewish ancestors with a mighty hand. It was not simply our ancestors who went forth, but all of us who have been freed from the bondage of idol worship and sin. We stand with those you have chosen to be a separate and peculiar people and to whom you have revealed your law and word.

BIRKAT HA-NER
Blessing Over the Candles

Leader: At sunset, to usher in the new day and to sanctify the seder, the lady of the house lights the candles with these blessings:

Hostess: *[Hostess may cover her head if desired. She recites the blessing in English as she lights the candles.]* May the festival lights we now kindle inspire us to use our gifts to spread your word and light to all the world. Use us, O God, to heal and not harm, to help and not hinder, to bless and not curse, to serve you O God, our rock and redeemer.

[Hostess covers her eyes and continues in Hebrew.]

מֶלֶךְ הָעוֹלָם, אֲשֶׁר קִדְּשָׁנוּ בְּיֵשׁוּעַ, אֲשֶׁר בִּשְׁמוֹ
בָּרוּךְ אַתָּה, יְיָ אֱלֹהֵינוּ,
מַדְלִיקִים אֲנַחְנוּ נֵר שֶׁל יוֹם טוֹב.

Ba-ruch a-tah A-do-nai, e-lo-hay-nu me-lech ha-o-lam, a-sher ki-de-sha-nu be-Y'shu-a, a-sher bish-mo mad-li-kim a-nach-nu ner shel yom tov.

Leader and Group: Blessed are you, O LORD our God, King of the universe, who has sanctified us in Y'shua, in whose name we light the [*on Sabbath:* Sabbath and] festival lights.

Blessed are you, O LORD our God, King of the universe, who has kept us alive and sustained us, and has brought us to this festive season.

Instructor: Let us remember the significance of the Passover seder, Messiah's last supper with his disciples. For he said, "I have eagerly desired to eat this Passover with you before I suffer. For I tell you, I will not eat it again until it finds fulfillment in the kingdom of God."

KADDESH
(Also referred to as Kiddush)
Sanctification of the Meal

Leader: The purging of leaven made the house holy, confession made each individual holy and the lighting of the festal candles made the day holy. Now the first cup of wine makes the meal holy.

THE FOUR CUPS

Leader: Though not commanded in Torah, the four cups are a very ancient tradition of the seder. They each relate to God's promises of freedom to our people. With each cup we remember his words found in Exodus 6:6-7:

The first cup is the Cup of Sanctification:

Group: "I will bring you out from under the yoke of the Egyptians."

Leader: The Cup of Deliverance:

Group: "I will free you from being slaves to them."

Leader: The Cup of Redemption:

Group: "I will redeem you with an outstretched arm and with mighty acts of judgment."

Leader: The Cup of Praise:

Group: "I will take you as My own people."

THE CUP OF SANCTIFICATION

Instructor: The word sanctification means "to separate." It is our faith in Y'shua, Messiah of Israel, which sanctifies us and separates us to live holy lives.

Leader: This is the first cup—the Cup of Sanctification. Let us take it together and proclaim the holiness of this day of deliverance.

בָּרוּךְ אַתָּה, יְיָ אֱלֹהֵינוּ, מֶלֶךְ הָעוֹלָם, בּוֹרֵא פְּרִי הַגָּפֶן.

Ba-ruch a-tah A-do-nai, e-lo-hay-nu me-lech ha-o-lam, bo-ray p'ree ha-ga-fen.

Leader and Group: "Blessed are you, O LORD our God, King of the universe, who makes the fruit of the vine."

Leader: Let us all drink this cup of sanctification.

[Each person drinks from his or her cup at the tables.]

15

*Adult #1: Blessed are you, O LORD our God, King of the universe, who has chosen us from all people, and lifted us up over all nations, and made us holy.

*Adult #2: And you have given us, O LORD our God, in love [*on the Sabbath:* Sabbath days for rest,] appointed times for rejoicing, festivals and festive seasons for joy, [*on the Sabbath:* this Sabbath and] this Festival of Unleavened Bread, anniversary of our freedom, [*on the Sabbath:* in love,] a holy assembly commemorating the Exodus from Egypt.

*Adult #3: For you have chosen us and made us holy above all people, and you have given us as an inheritance, [*on Sabbath:* the Sabbath and] your holy festivals [*on the Sabbath:* in love and favor,] with rejoicing and joy. Blessed are you, O LORD, who makes holy [*on the Sabbath:* the Sabbath,] Israel, the church and the festive seasons."

⋘⋗**URCHATZ**⋗⋘

Washing the Hands

Leader: Ancient regulation requires that hands must be washed before dipping food into any liquid. In the days when the Temple was standing, it was part of the process of purification to be holy unto the Lord. The purification process also included sacrifice because no amount of water could cleanse us from our sins. God said: "It is blood that makes atonement and without the shedding of blood there is no forgiveness" (Leviticus 17:11; Hebrews 9:22).

However, we are now free. Therefore, tonight in remembrance of that freedom, only the leader will wash and he [she] will do so without the ritual of prayer.

[The leader ceremonially washes his or her hands in the small bowl provided.]

Instructor: During the Last Supper, it might have been at this point that, as the leader of the house, Messiah prepared to wash, not his own hands, but the feet of his disciples! *[Instructor simulates washing the feet of a guest.]*

It is helpful to know that the tables of that time did not look like the famous painting of Leonardo da Vinci. Instead they were horseshoe shaped and were very close to the ground. Since there were no chairs then, people sat on the ground. On Passover, to demonstrate freedom, pillows were placed around the table and Jews would recline rather than sit upright.

From the events recorded in the Gospel of John, we know the seating arrangement at the Last Supper. Peter and John sat opposite each other—Peter was on the right end and John was on the left. Sitting next to John was Y'shua. Since everyone reclined on their left side, John was leaning on Y'shua's breast. Sitting on the other side of Y'shua was Judas. Surprisingly this was the place of honor.

John 13:4-5 records what happened: "He got up from the meal, took off his outer clothing, and wrapped a towel around his waist. After that, he poured water into a basin and began to wash his disciples' feet, drying them with the towel that was wrapped around him."

Remember who was sitting in the place of honor? Judas! So it would have been his feet that Y'shua washed first.

What a contrast to the argument that the disciples had just had regarding who would be the greatest in the kingdom of God. Messiah demonstrated that humiliation often comes before exaltation.

Men: Messiah said, "If anyone wants to be first, he must be the very last, and the servant of all" (Mark 9:35).

Women: And he said, "Now that I, your Lord and Teacher, have washed your feet, you also should wash one another's feet. I have set you an example that you should do as I have done for you" (John 13:14-15).

Instructor: Y'shua's washing the disciples' feet was only one act of his humility. "For though he was God, he laid aside his mighty power and glory, taking on the guise of a slave, becoming like men. He humbled himself even further by actually dying a criminal's death on the cross" (Philippians 2:5-8, Amplified).

Men: At the Last Supper, Jesus said, "Unless I wash you, you have no part of me."

Women: He also said, "You are clean, though not every one of you."

Group: For he knew who was going to betray him.

 KARPAS

Rebirth and Renewal
Eating the Greens

Leader: We praise you, God, sovereign of existence! You have called us for service from among the people and have hallowed

17

our lives with your Spirit. In love you preserved us and protected us through the dark times as well as the joyous times.

Leader and Group: I will sing to the LORD all my life; I will sing praise to my God as long as I live. Praise the LORD, O my soul. Praise the LORD *(Psalm 104:33, 35).*

Leader: The wine we drank was red in color, reminding us of the blood of the Passover lamb. These greens [leader holds up greens] remind us of the hyssop that applied this blood to the door-frames of the homes of the Hebrew slaves. The salt water [leader holds up salt water] reminds us of tears we shed in bondage and of the waters of the Red Sea through which we passed to safety. Let us dip the greens in salt water as we recite:

[Each person takes a sprig of green from the seder plate and dips it into the salt water and eats.]

Ba-ruch a-tah A-do-nai, e-lo-hay-nu me-lech ha-o-lam, bo-ray p'ree ha-a-da-mah.

Leader and Group: Blessed are you, O LORD our God, King of the universe, who creates the fruit of the earth.

Music: Song of your choice

YACHATZ

Breaking the Middle Matzoh
A Bond Formed by Sharing

[The leader uncovers the matzoh and lifts the matzoh container.]

Leader: The matzoh, or unleavened bread, that we use in the seder is kept in a linen container. The container has three compartments to hold three matzot, which symbolizes a unity or "echad." This is a compound unity—a whole consisting of several parts.

Instructor: There is no agreement as to why there are three matzot. Some say it symbolizes the priests, the Levites and the congregation. Others say it represents the three patriarchs: Abraham, Isaac and Jacob.

Believers in Y'shua can see that it could also represent the tri-unity of God: Father, Son and Spirit.

[The leader takes the middle matzoh and breaks it into two parts. He or she places the smaller part back between the two whole matzot in the container. Then he or she wraps the larger part in a napkin or bag. For larger groups, the host at each table should do this.]

Leader: We take the middle matzoh and break it in two. We then put the smaller piece back between the other two pieces and wrap the larger piece in a separate napkin. This larger piece is now called the afikoman, which means "dessert." We will hide the afikoman until after the meal. Later we will share it as the Passover offering was once shared in Jerusalem. Among people everywhere, the sharing of bread forms a bond of fellowship.

[Have all the children close their eyes while the leader hides the afikoman. It can be hidden in an easy-to-find location such as under the tablecloth or behind a curtain. For large groups, the host at each table should hide the afikoman for that table.]

[Leader holds up the matzoh container.] This is the bread of affliction, which our ancestors ate in the land of Egypt. Then we were slaves; now we are free! We celebrate Passover here, next year maybe in the land of Israel.

Instructor: The broken matzoh is also the symbol of the affliction suffered by Y'shua to bring us ultimate peace through faith in him.

Group: As freed men, let us share with all who are hungry. Let all who are lost or in want share the hope of Passover.

Leader: God humbled us and caused us to hunger in order to test us and to know our hearts. Then he fed us manna, the food of angels. He protected and provided for all our needs that we might understand that we do not live by bread alone, but by every word that comes out of the mouth of the LORD (Deuteronomy 8:3).

[The matzoh container is returned to its place, and the second cup is poured for all participants.]

Group: We give thanks unto the Lord. His mercies are new every morning. Great is his faithfulness.

❖MAGGID❖

Recounting the Story of the Exodus

Leader: This next section developed from the imperative of Exodus 12:26-27: "When your children ask you, 'What does this ceremony mean to you?' then tell them, 'It is the Passover sacrifice to the LORD, who passed over the houses of the Israelites in Egypt and spared our homes when he struck down the Egyptians.'"

The questions we are about to ask provide the opportunity to tell the story in a most dramatic way so that the past, present and future collide as we see God's hand upon us. Tonight's celebration is to be a living drama. It is not the record of a dead event, or an allegory. It is to be an act of personal identification.

*The Exodus event provided God's pattern of salvation. This pattern is repeated throughout the Scriptures. We see God in his infinite compassion and love stooped from the heavens to bring his people out of desperate trouble and to provide for them in a new and good environment:

*Adult #1: Bringing Israel out of bondage to Egypt and into the Land of Promise.

*Adult #2: Bringing Israel out of exile in Babylon and back into the Land.

*Adult #3: Bringing those who believe in Y'shua out from the kingdom of darkness and sin; bringing them into the kingdom of light and life.

*Adult #4: Bringing believers of all eras out of this cursed creation and into the new heavens and new earth.

THE FOUR QUESTIONS

Leader: Mah nish-ta-nah ha-lai-lah ha-zeh mi-kol ha-lay-lot?

Child #1: Why is this night different from all other nights? On all other nights we eat leavened *or* unleavened bread. Why on this night only matzoh—the unleavened bread?

Child #2: On all other nights we eat any kind of vegetable. Why on this night only maror—the bitter herbs?

Child #3: On all other nights we are not required to dip our vegetables even once. Why on this night two times?

Child #4: On all other nights we eat sitting upright *or* reclining. Why on this night do all recline?

Leader: The answers to these questions explain the major features of the seder: We were once slaves of Pharaoh in Egypt, but the LORD our God brought us out from there with a mighty hand and an outstretched arm. If the Holy One, blessed be he, had not brought our ancestors out from Egypt, then we, our children and their children would still be slaves to Pharaoh in Egypt. Therefore, even if we were all wise, all understanding, all experienced, all intimate with the Scriptures, we would still need to recount the Exodus from Egypt. And whoever recounts at length is praiseworthy.

Adult #1: On this night we eat only matzoh to remind us of the swiftness of God's salvation, which came so quickly there was no time for dough to rise. Further, the purging of leaven from our houses reminds us to purge our lives of sinful thoughts and actions.

*Instructor: Similarly, we eagerly wait for Messiah's swift return "as a thief in the night." And we seek to live holy lives so as "not to shrink away from him in shame at his coming."

Adult #2: On this night we eat maror to remind us of the bitterness of bondage in Egypt.

*Instructor: Similarly, as believers in Messiah we remember the bitterness of bondage to sin and death from which Messiah has freed us.

Adult #3: On this night we dip the greens into salt water to remind us of the tears shed in bondage. We dip the matzoh in the charoset to remind us of the sweetness of freedom, which the LORD brought about through the Exodus.

*Instructor: Similarly, as believers in Messiah we remember how he turned our tears of sadness into joy. We praise him for the abundant life into which he has brought us.

Adult #4: On this night we recline because in ancient times that was the posture of free people at meals. Those whom God liberated in the Exodus were no longer slaves.

*Instructor: Similarly, as believers in Messiah we know that we have been made new creations. We are freed from our past sin and pain, freed to live with joy in the present and freed to live and reign with God forever! Freed by Y'shua, we are free indeed.

*THE FOUR SONS

[Note: For a shorter service you can skip forward to page 25.]

*Leader: The Torah commands us to tell our children about the Exodus from Egypt. Four times the Torah repeats: "And you shall tell your child on that day. . . ." From this we can infer that what is called "The Four Sons" example illustrates four attitudes toward God's salvation as revealed in the Exodus and the Passover seder:

*Adult #1: In Deuteronomy 6:20, the wise son asks, "What is the meaning of the stipulations, decrees and laws the LORD our God has commanded?"

It is the wise one who wants to know the service that is his to do. He is to be instructed fully in the laws and traditions of the Passover. We are made wise as well by seeking the LORD our God through intimacy in prayer and in his Scriptures.

*Group: Instruct a wise man and he will be wiser still; teach a righteous man and he will add to his learning *(Proverbs 9:9).*

*Adult #2: The wicked son asks, "What does this service mean to you?" The wicked one withdraws himself from anything beyond self and thus from the joy of redemption.

Because of the way in which he says "to you," he excludes himself from the community. He is to be told, "This is done because of what the LORD my God did for me when I went forth from Egypt; had you been in Egypt with this attitude, you would not have been redeemed."

The wicked responds to God's offer of salvation through Y'shua the Messiah by considering it to be for others, rejecting it without considering Scripture.

*Group: The fool says in his heart, "There is no God." Salvation is far from the wicked, for they do not seek out your decrees *(Psalms 53:1, 119:155).*

*Adult #3: The innocent son, one not set in his ways, asks, "What does this mean?"

To the person of open simplicity, give a straightforward answer: for "the Torah of God makes wise the simple." He is to be told of the power and goodness of God's salvation, "With a mighty hand, the LORD brought us out of Egypt."

The young or unknowledgeable among us also need to hear of the power and goodness of God's salvation made available through faith in the Messiah today.

*Group: The unfolding of your words gives light; it gives understanding to the people *(Psalm 119:130)*.

*Leader: The son who does not know what to ask must be told clearly and carefully how the LORD has brought deliverance to Israel in the past and to us all in the present.

*Music: "El Shaddai" or a song of your choice.

*Leader: God brought our fathers from idolatry to his service, as Joshua 24:2-4 states: "Joshua said to all the people, 'This is what the LORD, the God of Israel, says: "Long ago your forefathers, including Terah the father of Abraham and Nahor, lived beyond the River and worshipped other gods. But I took your father Abraham from the land beyond the River and led him throughout Canaan and gave him many descendants. I gave him Isaac, and to Isaac I gave Jacob and Esau. I assigned the hill country of Seir to Esau, but Jacob and his sons went down to Egypt."'"

*Group: Blessed be the one who keeps his promise to Israel! For the holy one, blessed be he, planned the end of their bondage, to do as he had said to our father Abraham at the Covenant of the Pieces.

*Leader: "Know for certain that your descendants will be strangers in a country not their own, and they will be enslaved and mistreated four hundred years. But I will punish the nation they serve as slaves, and afterward they will come out with great possessions" (Genesis 15:13-14).

*Instructor: Similarly, those who are not genealogical descendants of Abraham—the Gentiles—can praise the LORD for his faithfulness to his covenant with Abraham in which he said, "And all peoples on earth will be blessed through you." For through the ultimate descendant of Abraham, Y'shua the Messiah, salvation has come to Israel, to the Gentiles and to the ends of the earth!

*Group: We give thanks to the LORD, for he is good. His love endures forever.

*Leader: When we were few in number we were strangers everywhere we went. We wandered from nation to nation, from one kingdom to another. He allowed no one to oppress us; for our sake he rebuked kings: "Do not touch my anointed ones: do my prophets no harm" (Psalm 105:12-15).

*Group: He remembers his covenant forever, the word he commanded, for a thousand generations *(Psalm 105:8).*

*Leader: He remembered the covenant he made with Abraham, the oath he swore to Isaac. He confirmed it to Jacob as a decree to Israel as an everlasting covenant *(Psalm 105:9-10).*

*Group: To you I will give the land of Canaan as the portion you will inherit.

*Leader: This promise has sustained our fathers and us. For in every generation men have risen up against us to destroy us. However, the holy one, blessed be he, has saved us from their hand.

*Group: Consider Laban, the Syrian.

*Leader: Laban tried to uproot all of Israel, as it is written in Deuteronomy 26:5, "My father was a Syrian, about to perish, and he went down to Egypt and sojourned there, few in number; and there he became a nation, great, mighty, and populous" *[NKJV].*

*Group: Israel did not go by choice, but by the hand of God. The people of Israel did not go to settle permanently, but only to dwell temporarily. For God had sent a famine on the land and destroyed all their supplies of food.

*Leader: As it is written in Genesis 47:4, the sons of Jacob said to Pharaoh: "We have come to live here awhile, because the famine is severe in Canaan and your servants' flocks have no pasture."

*Group: They didn't realize it, but God had sent a man before them—Joseph who was sold as a slave.

*Leader: They bruised his feet with shackles, they put his neck in irons until what he foretold came to pass. The word of the

LORD proved Joseph's word to be true *(Psalm 105:17-19)*.

> ***Group:** The king sent for Joseph and released him.

> ***Leader:** The king made Joseph master of his household, ruler over all the king possessed. He was to instruct the king's princes as he pleased and teach the king's elders wisdom *(Psalm 105:20-21)*.

> ***Group:** That is how it was when Israel entered Egypt. Jacob lived as an alien in the land of Ham.

> ***Leader:** They came as royal guests of Pharaoh.

> ***Group:** Joseph and all of the people of that generation died. However, the Lord made us to be fruitful and we multiplied and became exceedingly numerous. Israel filled the land *(Exodus 1:7)*.

[Note: Shorter services resume at this point.]

For shorter services only [longer services skip to bottom of this page]:
Leader: To experience the freedom of Passover, we must try to experience the affliction of Passover. However, the story of Passover doesn't begin in Egypt, but in Ur, a city in Mesopotamia.

Ur was a great city, a cultured city even by modern standards. The Chaldeans were a religious people and served many gods and idols.

Yet it was there that God spoke to a man named Abram (later to be called Abraham) and said, "Leave your country, your people and your father's household and go to the land I will show you. I will make your name great, and you will be a blessing. I will bless those who bless you and whoever curses you I will curse; and all peoples on earth will be blessed through you" (Genesis 21:1-3).

Therefore by faith Abram left as the Lord had told him, and he traveled to Canaan. Later God made those same promises to Isaac and to Jacob. Jacob became the father of 12 sons, the tribes of Israel.

Eventually there was a famine in the land and Jacob and his sons went down to Egypt to dwell—it was to be temporary. Israel was treated royally because of Joseph. Once sold into slavery, Joseph (who was one of Jacob's sons) was now master of the king's household, ruler over the king's possessions *(Psalm 105:2-21)*.

For all services:
Leader: Then a new king, who didn't know about Joseph, came to power. Instead of respecting Israel, this king feared their

increasing numbers. He declared, "Come we must deal shrewdly with them or they will become even more numerous and if war breaks out will join our enemies, fight against us and leave the country."

"So they put slavemasters over them to oppress them with forced labor and work them ruthlessly. They made their lives bitter . . ." (Exodus 1:11-14). When the Jewish people continued to multiply, the king ordered that every newborn boy be killed.

Group: In faithfulness to his promise, the LORD raised up a deliverer—his name was Moses.

Leader: Moses trained 40 years as a royal son in Egypt and 40 years as a shepherd in Midian. During this time, the Israelites groaned in their slavery and cried out—and God heard their cries.

Men: We cried out to the LORD, the God of our fathers. The LORD heard our voice and saw our misery, toil and oppression *(Deuteronomy 26:7)*.

Women: Then God remembered his covenant with Abraham, Isaac and Jacob.

Leader: So the LORD appeared to Moses at Mount Sinai, and revealed his character in his name, I AM—in Hebrew, YHWH. I AM YHWH the God who hears the groanings of his people, remembers his covenant with Abraham, with Isaac and with Jacob. The LORD God said to Moses, "I have indeed seen the misery of my people in Egypt. I have heard them cry out, and I am concerned about their suffering. So I have come down to rescue them from the hand of the Egyptians and to bring them out of that land into a good and spacious land." The LORD God then returned with Moses to battle with the "gods" of Egypt.

Men: Praise the LORD who brought us out of Egypt with a mighty hand and an outstretched arm,

Women: With great terror and with miraculous signs and wonders *(Deuteronomy 26:8)*.

Group: WE PRAISE THE LORD OUR GOD.

THE TEN PLAGUES

Instructor: This section of the seder is extremely important as it reflects God's intolerance of sin, especially pride, disobedience and unbelief. Through the prophet Ezekiel, God said, "The one who sins must die." As harsh as the plagues may seem to us, they remind us that "the wages of sin is death" (Ezekial 18:4; Romans 6:23).

Leader: The ten plagues that the LORD inflicted upon Egypt punished them for their harsh treatment of his people and humiliated their "gods." He showed his strength as the only true God of the universe.

Men: Though the plagues on Egypt were the result of their own evil, we do not rejoice over their defeat.

Women: Instead we recognize their suffering and express sorrow for their pain and loss.

Leader: A full cup of wine is a symbol of joy. Therefore as we recall the plagues and the destruction each one caused, we will lessen the amount of wine in our cups.

As each plague is mentioned, take a drop of wine from your cup and allow it to drip onto either your plate or a piece of matzoh.

Leader and Group:
The plague of blood *[dip and drip]*
Frogs *[dip and drip]*
Lice *[dip and drip]*
Flies *[dip and drip]*
Pestilence *[dip and drip]*
Boils *[dip and drip]*
Hail *[dip and drip]*
Locusts *[dip and drip]*
Darkness *[dip and drip]*
Slaying of the firstborn *[dip and drip]*

Leader: Let us also remember other plagues of the past and in the present.

Leader and Group:
The Holocaust *[dip and drip]*
Cancer *[dip and drip]*
AIDS *[dip and drip]*
*[Add a few modern-day plagues.]

27

Leader: O LORD, we ask for mercy and thank you for your deliverance from all these plagues.

*You sent darkness and made the land dark—for they had rebelled against your words.

*Group: You turned their water into blood, causing their fish to die.

*Leader: Their land teemed with frogs that went up into the bedrooms of their rulers.

*Group: You spoke, and there came swarms of flies and gnats throughout their country.

*Leader: You turned their rain into hail, with lightning throughout their land.

*Group: You struck down their vines and fig trees and shattered the trees of their country.

*Leader: You spoke and the locusts came, grasshoppers without number; they ate up every green thing in their land, ate up the produce of their soil.

*Group: Then you struck down all the firstborn in their land, the firstfruits of all their manhood.

*Leader: You brought out Israel, laden with silver and gold. From among their tribes no one faltered.

*Group: The Egyptians were glad when Israel left, because the dread of Israel had fallen on Egypt.

*Leader: You spread out a cloud as a covering for the people of Israel and a fire to give light at night.

*Group: They asked, and you brought them quail and satisfied them with the bread of heaven.

*Leader: You opened the rock, and water gushed out; like a river it flowed in the desert.

*Group: For you remembered your holy promise given to your servant Abraham.

Leader: You brought out your people with rejoicing, your chosen ones with shouts of joy. You gave them the lands of the nations that they might keep your precepts and observe your laws (Psalm 78).

Leader and Group: PRAISE THE LORD!

DAYENU

Leader: The song "Dayenu" answers the question, "For how many favors do we owe praise to God?" The answer is "unending." If the LORD had done any one of the mighty acts of the Exodus, that would have been enough for us or, in Hebrew, "Dayenu." However, the LORD continually saves and provides!

Music: "Dayenu" (It would have been enough for us)

[Sing the song on page 52 in unison. Then sing the following verses to the same melody. An alternative: The leader can recite the verses below and the group can sing the chorus after each verse is recited.]

Leader: If he had only brought us out of Egypt, but had not punished the Egyptians—Dayenu!

If he had only punished the Egyptians, but had not destroyed their gods—Dayenu!

If he had only destroyed their gods, but had not slain their firstborn—Dayenu!

If he had only slain their firstborn, but had not given us their wealth—Dayenu!

If he had only given us their wealth, but had not divided the sea for us—Dayenu!

If he had only divided the sea for us, but had not led us through on dry ground—Dayenu!

If he had only led us through on dry ground, but had not drowned our oppressors—Dayenu!

If he had only drowned our oppressors, but had not provided for us in the desert for forty years—Dayenu!

If he had only provided for us in the desert for forty years, but had not fed us with manna—Dayenu!

If he had only fed us with manna, but had not given us the Sabbath—Dayenu!

If he had only given us the Sabbath, but had not brought us to Mount Sinai—Dayenu!

If he had only brought us to Mount Sinai, but had not given us the Torah—Dayenu!

If he had only given us the Torah, but had not brought us into the Land of Israel—Dayenu!

If he had only brought us into the Land of Israel, but had not built us the Temple—Dayenu!

Instructor: All believers in Y'shua declare:

[Continue with the lyrics, which can either be recited by the leader or sung by the group.]

Had Messiah only come to show us how to live according to God's will, but had not died for our sins—Dayenu!

Had Messiah only died for our sins, but not raised to give us eternal life—Dayenu!

Had Messiah only been raised to give us eternal life, but not sent us His Spirit—Dayenu!

Had Messiah only sent us his Spirit, but was not coming to bring us into eternal fellowship with the Father—Dayenu!

Leader and Group: But he is coming!

[Sing chorus twice.]

THE THREE ESSENTIALS

Leader: Rabbi Gamaliel used to say, "Whoever does not explain the following three essentials of the Passover has not fulfilled his duty." These are pesach (the Passover lamb), matzoh (the unleavened bread) and maror (the bitter herbs).

[The leader lifts up the shankbone of the lamb.]

This represents the Passover lamb (pesach) that was slain. Its blood was put on our forefathers' doorposts that they might be saved. It reminds us that the holy one, blessed be he, passed over the houses of our forefathers in Egypt. As is said in the Torah (Exodus 12:27): "It is the Passover sacrifice to the LORD, who passed over the houses of the Israelites in Egypt and spared our homes when he struck down the Egyptians."

Instructor: It also reminds us of Y'shua, who was called "the Lamb which takes away the sin of the world." When, by faith, we apply his blood to our hearts, God's hand of judgment passes over our sins and we are saved.

[The leader lifts up the matzoh container.]

Leader: This matzoh reminds us that in their haste to flee, our ancestors did not have time to let their dough rise before the King of kings, the holy one who is blessed, revealed himself to them and redeemed them. The Torah (Exodus 12:39) states: "With the dough they had brought from Egypt, they baked cakes of unleavened bread. The dough was without yeast because they had been driven out of Egypt and did not have time to prepare food for themselves."

Instructor: The matzoh also reminds us of the perfect life of Y'shua. Though he was tempted in all ways, he did not sin.

[The leader lifts up the seder plate, which contains the maror.]

Leader: This maror reminds us that the Egyptians embittered the lives of our fathers in Egypt, as is said in the Torah (Exodus 1:14): "They made their lives bitter with hard labor in brick and mortar and with all kinds of work in the fields; in all their hard labor the Egyptians used them ruthlessly."

Instructor: We are also reminded that sin is the most ruthless of all taskmasters. Sin ensnares us, putting us in bondage to pain, fear, anxiety and, worst of all, it separates us from God. But faith in Y'shua frees us from the tyranny of sin. Along with the Psalmist and John, we can say, "The snare is broken and we are set free. Freed by the Son we are free indeed!" (Psalm 124:7; John 8:36).

Leader: In response to the mighty acts of the LORD, we respond with the full vocabulary of biblical praise.

Group: We are privileged to thank, to praise, to laud, to glorify, to exalt, to honor, to bless, to extol and give reverence to you, O Lord our God, who performed all these miracles for our ancestors and for us. You have brought us forth from slavery to freedom, from sorrow to joy, from mourning to festivity, from darkness to light and from bondage to redemption! Therefore, we sing to you a new song! Hallelujah!

Music: A praise song of your choice.

Leader: We now turn to the first part of the Hallel, Psalms 113 and 114. Praise the LORD! Praise, O servants of the LORD.

Group: Praise the name of the LORD!

Leader: Let the name of the LORD be praised, both now and forevermore. From the rising of the sun to the place where it sets . . .

Group: . . . the name of the LORD is to be praised.

Leader: The LORD is exalted over all the nations. His glory is above the heavens. Who is like the LORD our God, the one who sits enthroned on high, who stoops down to look on the heavens and the earth?

Group: He raises the poor from the dust and lifts the needy from the ash heap; he seats them with princes, with the princes of their people.

Leader and Group: Praise the LORD.

Leader: When Israel came out of Egypt, the house of Jacob from a people of foreign tongue, Judah became God's sanctuary, Israel his dominion.

Group: The sea looked and fled, the Jordan turned back! The mountains skipped like rams, the hills like lambs!

Leader: Why was it, O sea, that you fled, O Jordan, that you turned back, you mountains, that you skipped like rams, you hills, like lambs?

Group: Tremble, O earth, at the presence of the Lord, at the presence of the God of Jacob who turned the rock into a pool, the hard rock into springs of water!

THE CUP OF DELIVERANCE

Leader: The Cup of Deliverance is based on YHWH's second promise to Israel in Exodus 6:6, "I will free you (in Hebrew *natsl* or tear you away) from your slavery."

Instructor: In the same way, Y'shua has freed us, or torn us away from the kingdom of darkness and brought us into the kingdom of light *(Colossians 1:13).*

Leader: Let us raise the second cup, the Cup of Deliverance. [Raise the second cup, the Cup of Deliverance.] Blessed are you, O LORD our God, who redeemed us and brought us to this night. So, O LORD, will you bring us to other festivals, and into your new city. You have put a new song into our hearts, a song of praise and thanksgiving for our redemption and the liberation of our souls. Blessed are you, O LORD, redeemer of Israel and all nations.

בָּרוּךְ אַתָּה, יְיָ אֱלֹהֵינוּ, מֶלֶךְ הָעוֹלָם, בּוֹרֵא פְּרִי הַגָּפֶן.

Ba-ruch a-tah A-do-nai, e-lo-hay-nu me-lech ha-o-lam, bo-ray p'ree ha-ga-fen.

Leader and Group: Blessed are you, O LORD our God, King of the universe, who makes the fruit of the vine.
Thank you for declaring us righteous and delivering us from your judgment and wrath.

[All drink from the second cup.]

Music: Song of your choice.

⤜➤ RACHTZAH ⤛➤
Washing the Hands

Leader: We all wash our hands now in preparation for the eating of the Passover elements.

[All the participants symbolically wash their hands.]

Leader: Blessed are you, O LORD our God, King of the universe, who has commanded us to eat the Passover. As we remember the plagues that fell upon the Egyptians, we know that your wrath will fall upon those who reject you.

Instructor: God's wrath will fall upon those who hear the truth, yet turn away. Even in the midst of the 12 who were closest to the Messiah, one was about to betray him as they celebrated Passover with the Last Supper.
Messiah declared his disciples clean after he washed their feet. He also said, "I am not referring to all of you, I know those I have chosen."

Men: "This is to fulfill the Scripture: He who shares my bread has lifted up his heel against me."

Women: "I am telling you now before it happens, so that when it does, you will believe that I am He."

Group: "I tell you, one of you is going to betray me" *(John 13:18, Psalm 41:9).*

Instructor: Remember the seating arrangement at the Last Supper. Peter sat at the right side of the horseshoe-shaped table. Across from him sat John, at the right hand of Y'shua. Judas was at the left hand of Y'shua. When Peter asked about the betrayer, he leaned across the table and said to John, "Ask him which one he means." Leaning back against Y'shua, John asked, "Lord who is it?" Y'shua answered, "It is the one to whom I will give this piece of bread when I have dipped it in the dish."

MOTZI, MATZOH, MAROR, KORECH

Leader: We have heard about the three elements, let us now share them together. First the matzoh *[Leader raises the matzoh* *container]:* Ba-ruch a-tah A-do-nai, e-lo-hay-nu me-lech ha-o-lam, ha-mo-tzee le-chem min ha-a-retz.

Leader and Group: Blessed are you, O LORD our God, King of the universe, who brings forth bread from the earth.

[The leader breaks olive-sized pieces from the upper and middle matzot and distributes them to all participants. For large groups the host at each table distributes the pieces.]

Leader: Ba-ruch a-tah A-do-nai, e-lo-hay-nu me-lech ha-o-lam, a-sher ki-de-sha-nu be-mitz-vo-tav, ve-tzi-va-nu al a-chi-lat ma-tzoh.

Leader and Group: Blessed are you, O LORD our God, King of the universe, who has commanded us to eat unleavened bread.

[All eat the matzoh.]

Leader: As it is commanded in Torah, let us remember the bitterness of slavery in Egypt by eating the maror.

Instructor: Remember what Messiah had said about the betrayer? It would be "the one to whom I will give this piece of bread when I have dipped it in the dish," the one sitting next to him at the place of honor, who would betray him. Let us now continue. . . .
[The leader now breaks the bottom matzoh into thin pieces for dipping in the maror. He dips each piece and then distributes to all. For large groups, the host at each table distributes the pieces.]

Leader: Ba-ruch a-tah A-do-nai, e-lo-hay-nu me-lech ha-o-lam, a-sher ki-de-sha-nu be-mitz-vo-tav, ve-tzi-va-nu al a-chi-lat ma-ror.

Leader and Group: Blessed are you, O LORD our God, King of the universe, who has commanded us to eat the maror.

[All eat.]

Instructor: "Judas took the bread. He went out, and it was night" (John 13:30).

Leader: Following the custom of Hillel, another great rabbi of Y'shua's time, we combine the elements together. This is meant to fulfill the commandment, "They shall eat the paschal lamb with matzoh and maror together."

*[The leader now breaks two pieces of matzoh for each partici-
pant from what is left of the matzoh. Each person then makes a sand-
wich using the maror and charoset. For large groups, the host at each
table distributes the pieces.]*

Group: Blessed are you, O Lord our God, who turns our
mourning into dancing.

Leader: *[Lifting the roasted egg.]* The roasted egg reminds
us of the final destruction of the Temple in 70 AD. We mourn its loss
as we remember God's words in Torah, "It is the blood that makes
atonement for one's life" (Leviticus 17:11) and God's words in the
New Covenant, "Without the shedding of blood there is no forgiveness
of sin" (Hebrews 9:22).

Instructor: The blood of animals could only cover and not
cleanse our sins. Y'shua the Lamb of God was the ultimate Passover
sacrifice. His was the perfect sacrifice of atonement, which could
bring peace and fellowship with God.

Leader: The egg also reminds us of the second Passover offering, called the "Hagigah." It was a voluntary act of worship that indicated the worshipers' desire to have peace and fellowship with God.

Instructor: Let us eat the egg as our "fellowship offering"
and remember that we are all called to make our lives living sacrifices
as we serve and follow God. To remind us that the joy of sacrifice may
be surrounded by tears, we dip the egg into the salt water before us.

[Everyone dips the egg into the salt water and eats.]

Leader: The meal will now be served . . . let's eat.

⋘SHULCHAN ORECH⋙
The Table Is Spread

*[After dinner, the group should spend some time singing. If
possible, and appropriate for your group, include one or two simple
Hebrew dances. The following is read when the group has settled back.]*

Instructor: At this point it is good to remind ourselves that
we are celebrating Passover with a fuller revelation than our ancestors
had when they celebrated it. We experience the celebration with the

knowledge of the complete canon of Scripture.

Imagine how the disciples might have felt as they experienced the Passover rituals as they had throughout their Jewish lives, but with growing confusion. They had seen the miracles their master had done, greater than those of Moses. They had heard the shouts of adoration of the people as they had walked with him into Jerusalem just four days before. Yet, the master was again talking about leaving them.

Imagine what thoughts Messiah might have had. This was his last dinner with his disciples. He had so much to tell them. They had been blinded by their own understanding of freedom. Had he not warned them about this trip to Jerusalem?

"We are going up to Jerusalem, and everything that is written by the prophets about the Son of Man will be fulfilled. He will be betrayed and handed over to the chief priests and the teachers of the law. They will condemn him to death and will turn him over to the Gentiles to be mocked and flogged and crucified" (Matthew 20:18-19; Luke 18:31-32).

As with so many people today, the disciples had forgotten the teachings of the law, the prophets and the Psalms. Messiah would have to suffer and rise from the dead for the remission of sins.

A DRAMATIC READING
Psalm 22 and Isaiah 53 Written for Three Voices

Adult #1: He grew up before him like a tender shoot and like a root out of dry ground. He had no beauty or majesty to attract us to him, nothing in his appearance that we should desire him.

He was despised and rejected by men, a man of sorrows, and familiar with suffering. As one from whom men hide their faces, he was despised, and we esteemed him not.

Adult #2: My God, my God, why have you forsaken me? Why are you so far from saving me, so far from the words of my groaning? I cry out, but you do not answer. Yet you are enthroned as the holy one, the praise of Israel. In you our fathers put their trust; they trusted and you delivered them. In you they trusted and were not disappointed.

But I am a worm and not a man, scorned by men and despised by the people. All who see me mock me, they hurl insults, shaking their heads: "He trusts in the LORD; let the LORD rescue him."

Adult #1: We all, like sheep, have gone astray, each of us has turned to his own way and the LORD has laid on him the iniquity of us all.

Adult #2: Do not be far from me, for trouble is near and there is no one to help.

Adult #1: Surely he took up our infirmities and carried our sorrows, yet we considered him stricken by God, smitten by him, and afflicted. But he was pierced for our transgressions; he was crushed for our iniquities.

Adult #2: I am poured out like water, and all my bones are out of joint. My heart is turned to wax; it has melted away within me.

Adult #1: He was oppressed and afflicted, yet he did not open his mouth; he was led like a lamb to the slaughter.

Adult #2: They divide my garments among them and cast lots for my clothing.

Adult #1: He was assigned a grave with the wicked, though he had done no violence, nor was any deceit in his mouth.

Adult #2: O LORD, be not far off; O my strength, come quickly to help me. Deliver my life from the power of the dogs.

Adult #1: Yet it was the LORD's will to crush him, to cause him to suffer and to make his life a guilt offering.
After the suffering of his soul he will see the light of life and be satisfied; by his knowledge my righteous servant will justify many.

Adult #3: You who fear the LORD, praise him! For he has not despised or disdained the suffering of the afflicted one; he has not hidden his face from him but has listened to his cry for help.
The poor will eat and be satisfied; they who seek the LORD will praise him. All the ends of the earth will remember and turn to the LORD. All the families of the nations will bow down before him. Posterity will serve him; future generations will be told about the LORD. They will proclaim his righteousness to a people yet unborn.

Adult #1: He has done it! He bore the sin of many and made intercession for the transgressors. The punishment that brings us peace was upon him and by his stripes we are healed!

Music: "He Paid Too High a Price" or "Via Dolorosa" or "Were You There?" or a song of your choice.

* * * * * * * * * * * *

Instructor: As Messiah celebrated Passover, he knew what was before him—the pain and also the glory. And he knew that before the day was over, he'd be abandoned by all of his disciples. They would be discouraged and afraid. In his infinite love and mercy he sought to challenge and to comfort them.

The words he spoke are as much for us today as they were for the disciples.

*Adult #1: Do not let your hearts be troubled. Trust in God; trust also in me. I am going to my father's house to prepare a place for you that you may be where I am.

*Adult #2: I am the way and the truth and the life. No one comes to the Father except through me.

*Adult #3: I will not leave you orphans. In my name, the Father will send another counselor. He will live with you and in you. He will teach you all things and will remind you of everything I have said to you.

*Adult #4: A time is coming when they will put you out of the synagogue, thinking they are offering a service to God. They will do such things because they have not known the Father or me.

*Adult #1: If the world hates you, keep in mind that it hated me first. They will treat you this way because of my name for they do not know the one who sent me. The world must learn that I do exactly what my Father has commanded me.

*Adult #2: He who hates me hates my Father as well. He who loves me, my Father will love. We will come to him and make our home with him.

*Adult #3: I have told you this that you will not go astray. When the time comes you will remember that I warned you.

*Adult #4: If you love me, you will obey my teaching. He who does not love me will not obey my teaching. These words you hear are not my own; they belong to the Father who sent me.

Men: A new command I give you, love one another. By this all will know that you are my disciples.

Women: I have told you these things so that in me you may have peace.

Instructor: Peace I leave with you, my peace I give to you. I do not give to you as the world gives.

Men: In the world you will have trouble.

Women: But take heart.

Group: I have overcome the world.

Instructor: Y'shua could offer his peace for he knew the victory that would be his. They would kill him, but on the third day the Son of Man would rise again; he would be raised to life!

⋙⋘ TZAPHUN ⋙⋘

Retrieving of the Afikoman, the Hidden Matzoh

[Retrieving the afikoman is a treat for the children. Allow about five minutes for all the Afikomans to be found. The adults should encourage the children by letting them know if they are getting close or far away. Each child should then hold the afikoman for a "ransom," which the child will negotiate with the host at the child's table. The ransom can be a small amount of money or some candy. The service cannot continue until all the Afikomans have been redeemed.]

[Pour the third cup of wine.]

Instructor: This next portion of the seder has immense significance for the believer in Messiah. It is here that we see a remarkable illustration of the truth spoken about the suffering servant by the prophet Isaiah.

The afikoman *[holding the afikoman]* is the middle piece of the three matzot that has been kept in the container, which forms a unity or "echad." It was broken, hidden away and brought back. For its redemption a ransom had to be paid.

In like manner Messiah, the second person of the triune God (whom Moses had also called echad) was broken, buried and brought back to life.

Leader: *[Distributes a piece of the afikoman to each person. For large groups, the host at each table distributes the pieces.]* The afikoman is our dessert. Its taste is to remain in our mouths as long as possible to remind us of all God's deliverance in the past, in the present and in the future.

Instructor: As he had done earlier, Y'shua took the bread and gave thanks.

Leader: Ba-ruch a-tah A-do-nai, e-lo-hay-nu me-lech ha-o-lam, ha-mo-tzee le-chem min ha-a-retz.

Group: Blessed are you, O LORD our God, King of the universe, who brings forth bread from the earth.

Instructor: But then he gave a new commandment, one that must have startled the disciples. He broke the bread and said, "Take, eat, this is my body, given for you; do this in remembrance of me."

[All eat the afikoman.]

Music: "Passover Lamb" or song of your choice.

⤙🙥 BARECH 🙥⤚

Blessing for the Meal

Leader: Here we give thanks after the meal to remind us that all that we have just enjoyed has come from and through the provision of God. We must be aware that his goodness and bounty are constant, daily occurrences and will always be so.
*As Moses gave thanks for the manna, we also thank God for our food; as Joshua gave thanks for the land flowing with milk and honey, we give thanks for the promised land.

Instructor: As David gave thanks for God's salvation, we too give thanks for Messiah; and as the prophets gave thanks for Jerusalem and the promises for freedom, so do we give thanks for the New Jerusalem.

Leader: Let us bless you, our God, of whose gifts we have partaken.

Group: Blessed are you, our God, by whose goodness we exist and by whose loving kindness we will have eternal life.

Leader: Blessed are you, our God, King of the universe, who feeds the whole world with your goodness, and with grace, kindness and mercy. For your mercy endures forever.

Group: We will give thanks unto you, O God, for having caused our ancestors to inherit that desirable, good and ample land and because you have brought us forth from the land of Egypt and redeemed us from the house of bondage.

Leader: We thank you for your covenant, your commandments and your love. Your mercy endures forever.

Instructor: As believers in Y'shua we thank you, O God, for Messiah Y'shua. We thank you that you have cleansed us and forgiven us of all our sin so that we can stand before you without fear. We thank you for your promise to never leave or forsake us but to return and bring us to your New Jerusalem where we will dwell in your house forever.

Leader: Up to this point we have focused on God's past redemption—how he brought us out from the land of Egypt and bondage and into the promised land of peace and freedom. In the remaining part of the Seder, our focus will be on God's future work of redemption. We will look at the time of Messiah's kingdom, a time of everlasting peace and freedom, even freedom from the influence of sin.

THE CUP OF REDEMPTION

Leader: The third cup, the Cup of Redemption, recalls God's third promise to Moses: "I will redeem you (in Hebrew *ga'al*) with an outstretched arm."

Instructor: A *ga'al* is one who pays a ransom for the life of another. He who redeemed our fathers from Egypt has redeemed us with his own blood.

Group: No man can redeem the life of another or give to God a ransom for him—the ransom for a life is costly, no payment is ever enough *(Psalm 49:7-8)*.

Leader: But God will redeem our lives from the grave. He will take us to himself *(Psalm 49:15)*.

Group: The LORD redeems his servants; no one will be

42

condemned who takes refuge in him *(Psalm 34:22)*.

Leader: The LORD is my rock and my redeemer.

Instructor: He became their savior. In all their distress he too was distressed. In his love and mercy he redeemed them (Isaiah 63:8-9).

Leader: We look forward to the final redemption promised in the new covenant: "I will put my law in their minds and write it on their hearts. I will be their God, and they will be my people.
"No longer will a man teach his neighbor, or a man his brother, saying 'Know the Lord,' because they will all know me, from the least of them to the greatest," declares the LORD. "For I will forgive their wickedness and will remember their sins no more" (Jeremiah 31:33-34).

[Everyone raises the third cup, the Cup of Redemption.]

Group: I know that my redeemer lives.

Instructor: To confirm the covenant at Mt. Sinai, Moses took the blood of the sacrifice offerings and sprinkled it on the people. As recorded in Exodus 24:8, he said, "This is the blood of the covenant that the LORD has made with you."
As the Last Supper was celebrated, Messiah was about to confirm the new covenant with his blood. Now the Cup of Redemption becomes our "thank offering."
Over this cup the Master once again gave new meaning to the existing ritual. As we have over the other cups and as Y'shua did at the Last Supper, we again give thanks.

Leader: Ba-ruch a-tah A-do-nai, e-lo-hay-nu me-lech ha-o-lam, bo-ray p'ree ha-ga-fen.

Group and Leader: Blessed are you, O LORD our God, King of the universe, who makes the fruit of the vine.

Instructor: Then Y'shua said, "Drink from it, all of you. This is my blood of the new covenant, which is poured out for many for the forgiveness of sins" (Matthew 26:27b-28).

[All drink from the third cup.]

Music: Song of your choice.

ELIJAH'S PLACE

Leader: Notice that a place has been set at the table but not used. It has been set for Elijah whose return before the coming of Messiah was proclaimed by the prophet Malachi: "See, I will send you the prophet Elijah before that great and dreadful day of the LORD comes. He will turn the hearts of the fathers to their children, and the hearts of the children to their fathers; or else I will come and strike the land with a curse" *(Malachi 4:5-6).*

As we celebrate our freedom from Egypt, we look toward the time when the whole world lives in peace. The nations will beat their swords into pruning hooks, the wolf will lie with the lamb and all the world will praise the Lord God of Israel.

Instructor: Elijah was to warn the people of God's judgment and to prepare the people for the coming Messiah. We know that Elijah's work was already accomplished in John the Baptiser. Nevertheless, we keep Elijah's place as a reminder of Messiah's next coming and of the many people who do not know him. It is to them we must bring the message of true redemption. For not only will Messiah bring peace, but he will also bring wrath upon all those who do not know him.

Our Jewish brethren open the door so that the prophet may enter. They wait breathlessly to see if he will indeed herald the coming of Messiah. However, we open the door to show our trust and dependence upon God and to alert our oppressors and the lost of his coming.

[Either a child or an adult opens a door, preferably one leading outside. Keep it open until the following liturgy is completed.]

*Leader: You are forgiving and good, O LORD, abounding in love to all who call to you. But you will pour forth your wrath upon the nations that do not recognize you, and upon the kingdoms that do not invoke your name.

Leader: Not unto us, O LORD! Not unto us, but to your name be the glory, because of your love and faithfulness.

Group: Why do the nations say, "Where is their God?" Our God is in heaven; he does whatever pleases him.

Leader: You who fear him, trust in the LORD—he is your help and shield.

Group: The LORD remembers us and will bless us; he will bless the house of Israel. He will bless the house of Aaron. He will bless those who fear the LORD—small and great alike.

[Shut the door.]

Music: "Eliyahu Ha-navi"

⊰⊱HALLEL⊰⊱

Songs of Praise

Instructor: Psalms 115-118 are the remaining Psalms in the Hallel. Y'shua and his disciples were probably singing these Psalms as they left the Upper Room.

Imagine how Y'shua might have felt as he sang these Psalms. The words were written for him and by him before the foundation of time. They are words of victory and of surrender. The Hallel was the perfect libretto as Messiah moved to the cross. On the way to Gethsemane, now only hours before his crucifixion, Y'shua sang the words of joy, of love and of trust in God.

Leader: Let us praise the LORD our God YHWH who hears and acts on our behalf. We join with our ancestors who sang the Hallel at every festival while the Temple was standing.

I love the LORD, for he heard my cry for mercy. Because he turned his ear to me, I will call on him as long as I live.

Group: The cords of death entangled me, I was overcome by trouble and sorrow.

Leader: Then I called on the name of the LORD.

Leader and Group: "O LORD, save me!"

Leader: LORD you are gracious and righteous.

Group: LORD you are full of compassion. When I was in great need, you saved me.

Leader and Group: Be at rest once more, O my soul, for the LORD has been good to you.

Leader: You O LORD have delivered my soul from death,

Group: My eyes from tears,

Leader: My feet from stumbling that I may walk before you LORD in the land of the living.

Group: How can we repay you LORD for all your goodness to us? We will lift up the Cup of Salvation and call on your name, LORD.

Leader: We will fulfill our vows to you in the presence of all your people.

Group: O LORD, truly I am your servant. You have freed me from my chains.

Leader: We will sacrifice a thank offering to you in the presence of your people,

Group: And in the courts of the house of the LORD.

Leader and Group: Praise you LORD!

Leader: Thank you LORD. You are good.

Group: Your love endures forever.

Leader: Let Israel say:

Group: His love endures forever.

Leader: Let those who fear the LORD say:

Group: His love endures forever.

Leader: In my anguish I cried to the LORD, and he answered me by setting me free.

Group: The LORD is with me.

Leader: I will not be afraid. What can man do to me? The LORD is with me, he is my helper.

Leader and Group: I will look with triumph on my enemies. I was pushed back and about to fall, but the LORD helped me.

Leader: The LORD is my strength and my song. He has become my salvation.

Group: I will not die but live, and will proclaim what the LORD has done.

Leader: Open the gates of righteousness; I will enter and give thanks, for he has become my salvation.

Group: The stone the builders rejected has become the capstone.

Leader: The LORD has done this, and it is marvelous in our eyes.

Leader and Group: This is the day the LORD has made, let us rejoice and be glad in it!

Leader: O LORD save us; O LORD grant us success.

Group: O LORD save us; O LORD grant us success.

Leader: Blessed is he who comes in the name of the LORD.

Group: Blessed is he who comes in the name of the LORD.

Leader: The LORD is God, and he has made his light shine upon us.

Group: With boughs in hand, join in the festal procession up to the horns of the altar.

Leader: You are my God, and I will give you thanks.

Group: You are my God, and I will exalt you.

Leader: Give thanks to the LORD, for he is good.

Leader and Group: His love endures forever.

THE CUP OF PRAISE
[Pour the fourth cup]

Leader: We now come to the fourth cup, the Cup of Praise, also called the Cup of the Kingdom. This cup is based on God's fourth promise in Exodus 6:7: "I will take you as my people and I will be your God."

Instructor: The disciples drank, thinking the time had come for their master to march triumphantly into Jerusalem. But Messiah knew there was another cup from which he had to drink. He did not drink from this one. Instead he said, "I tell you, I will not drink of this fruit of the vine from now until that day when I drink it anew with you in my Father's kingdom." As we drink, may we look forward to the day of Messiah's return. In that day there will be a better feast: the wedding banquet to which all who know, trust and worship Y'shua have been invited.

[All raise the fourth cup.]

Leader: In praise of the salvation the LORD has brought and that which is yet to come, we raise the fourth cup and recite in Hebrew: Ba-ruch a-tah A-do-nai, e-lo-hay-nu me-lech ha-o-lam, bo-ray p'ree ha-ga-fen.

Leader and Group: Blessed are you, O LORD our God, King of the universe, who makes the fruit of the vine.

[All drink.]

Leader: Blessed are you O LORD, God of Israel, God of our fathers. We praise you for who you are and all the mighty deeds your hand has done.

Group: Your love endures forever.

Leader: At your command the earth and its fullness was created. At your voice the seas parted for those who believed in you. For your goodwill and pleasure you redeemed Israel and sanctified it to be a holy nation of priests to serve you.

Group: Your love endures forever.

Leader: You also redeemed those who worshiped idols, calling your own a people who formerly were not called your people.

Group: Your love endures forever.

Leader: You alone are worthy to be praised. You are faithful when we are not. Your mercies are new every morning. Daily you load us with blessings.

Instructor: Blessed are you, O LORD our God, who has given us the gifts of salvation and eternal life.

Group: And this is eternal life, that we might know you, the one true God and Messiah Y'shua whom you sent.

Instructor: We look beyond your promise for a restored Israel *to* your promise of a new heaven and new earth. May the time not be distant O LORD when we might dwell in the New Jerusalem. In that day every knee shall bow and every tongue confess that Messiah is LORD. You will wipe away every tear. There will be no more death or mourning or crying or pain, for the old order of things will pass away. We will proclaim with the heavenly hosts:

Group: Worthy is the lamb who was slain. Salvation belongs to our God, who sits on the throne, and to the lamb.

Instructor: Amen! Praise and glory and wisdom and thanks and honor and power and strength be to our God forever and ever. Amen!

⊰≫·NIRTZAH·≪⊱

Leader: The order of the Passover service is now complete in accordance with all its laws, ordinances and statutes. Just as we were privileged to perform it, so may we be privileged to do it in the future.

Instructor: He is alive! Death could not hold Y'shua. According to all the Hebrew Scriptures, the Passover lamb was sacrificed, was buried and then rose again. He is coming back to bring us where he is. Expectantly we wait for that great Passover.

Leader: O pure one who dwells on high, raise up your numberless congregation! Soon, and with rejoicing, lead the offshoots of the stock that you have planted, the redeemed, to Zion!

Le-sha-nah ha-ba-ah bee-ru-sha-la-yeem ha-be-nu-yah!

Leader and Group: Next year in the rebuilt Jerusalem!

Music: "Medley of Praise"

REJOICE! This book is an adventure. It begins with Jewish people in captivity in Egypt and ends in triumph as the Hebrews enter the Promised Land.

REJOICE! This adventure is not only for those who are born Jewish, but also for every person who by accepting the Messiah as Lord has been born again.

REJOICE! We have been part of God's rescue from Egypt. He has led each believer in Y'shua into his or her own Canaan via the Cross.

Eliyahu Ha-Navi

E - li - ya - hu ha - na - vi E - li -

ya - hu ha - tish - bi E - li - ya - hu E - li -

ya - hu E - li - ya - hu ha - gil - a - di.

Bim - he - rah v' - ya - mei - nu ya - vo e -

lei - nu im Ma - shi - ach ben Da - vid

im Ma - shi - ach ben Da - vid.

אֵלִיָהוּ הַנָבִיא, אֵלִיָהוּ הַתִּשְׁבִּי, אֵלִיָהוּ, אֵלִיָהוּ, אֵלִיָהוּ הַגִּלְעָדִי,
בִּמְהֵרָה בְיָמֵינוּ יָבֹא אֵלֵינוּ עִם מָשִׁיחַ בֶּן דָוִד, עִם מָשִׁיחַ בֶּן דָוִד.

Elijah the prophet, Elijah the Tishbite, Elijah the Gileadite.
May he come quickly, in our days, with the Messiah, the son of David.

Dayenu

I - lu ho - tzi ho - tzi - a - nu ho - tzi - a - nu
I - lu na - tan na - tan la - nu na - tan la - nu
I - lu sha - lach sha - lach la - nu sha - lach la - nu

mi - mitz - ra - yim ho - tzi - a - nu mi - mitz - ra - yim
et ha - to - rah na - tan la - nu et ha - to - rah
et Ma - shi - ach sha - lach la - nu et Ma - shi - ach

da - ye - nu. Da - da - ye - nu
da - ye - nu. Da - da - ye - nu
da - ye - nu. Da - da - ye - nu

da - da - ye - nu da - da - ye - nu da-
da - da - ye - nu da - da - ye - nu da-
da - da - ye - nu da - da - ye - nu da-

ye - nu da - ye - nu da - ye - nu da - da -
ye - nu da - ye - nu da - ye - nu da - na -
ye - nu da - ye - nu da - ye - nu da - na -

ye - nu da - da - ye - nu
ye - nu da - da - ye - nu
ye - nu da - da - ye - nu

da - da - ye - nu da - ye - nu da - ye - nu.
da - da - ye - nu da - ye - nu da - ye - nu.
da - da - ye - nu da - ye - nu da - ye - nu.

If God had just brought us out of Egypt and done nothing more,
it would have been enough for us. If God had just given us the Torah
and done nothing more, it would have been enough for us. If God
had just sent the Messiah to us and done nothing more, it would have
been enough for us.

Eternally Grateful

Words and Music by
Janie-sue Wertheim

1. I am e - ter - nal - ly grate-ful to Je - sus for all He has done for me. He has gi - ven me life and sal - va-tion, gi - ven me li - ber - ty.
2. I will lift up the cup of sal - va-tion and call u - pon His name, through His blood I have re - demp-tion, a brand new life I claim.
3. Bless the Lord, bless the Lord O my soul and all that's with-in my frame, join and sing out the prais-es of Je - sus; e - ter - nal for e - ver the same.

O Lord I praise and I bless your name; give the glo-ry to you, (to you.) My heart, my soul they're in your hands, teach me to wor - ship you.

Passover Lamb

Words and Music by
Stuart Dauermann and Sam Nadler

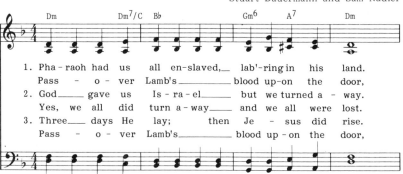

1. Pha - raoh had us all en-slaved,__ lab'-ring in his land.
   Pass - o - ver Lamb's_____ blood up-on the door,
2. God____ gave us Is - ra - el____ but we turned a - way.
   Yes, we all did turn a-way___ and we all were lost.
3. Three____ days He lay; then Je - sus did rise.
   Pass - o - ver Lamb's_____ blood up - on the door,

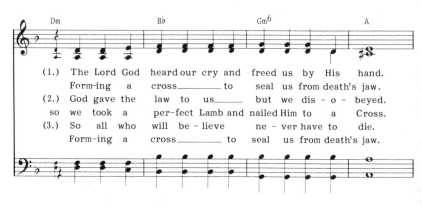

(1.) The Lord God heard our cry and freed us by His hand.
Form-ing a cross_____ to seal us from death's jaw.
(2.) God gave the law to us____ but we dis - o - beyed.
so we took a per-fect Lamb and nailed Him to a Cross.
(3.) So all who will be - lieve ne - ver have to die.
Form-ing a cross_____ to seal us from death's jaw.

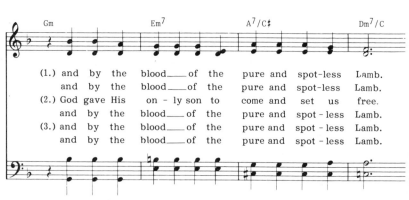

(1.) and by the blood___of the pure and spot-less Lamb.
and by the blood___of the pure and spot-less Lamb.
(2.) God gave His on - ly son to come and set us free.
and by the blood___of the pure and spot - less Lamb.
(3.) and by the blood___of the pure and spot - less Lamb.
and by the blood___of the pure and spot - less Lamb.

Chad Gadya

רַד גַּדְיָא, חַד גַּדְיָא.

One kid, one kid.

Additional English verses for Chad Gadya:

Then came a dog and bit the cat, then came a cat and ate the kid that my father bought for two zuzim, chad gadya, chad gadya.

Then came a stick and beat the dog, then came a dog and bit the cat,...

Then came a fire and burned the stick, then came a stick and beat the dog,...

Then came water and put out the fire, then came a fire and burned the stick,...

Then came an ox and drank up the water, then came water and put out the fire,...

Then came the butcher and butchered the ox, then came an ox and drank up the water,...

Then came the Angel of Death and slaughtered the butcher, then came the butcher and butchered the ox,....

Then came the Holy One, blessed be He, and slaughtered the Angel of Death, then came the Angel of Death and slaughtered the butcher,...